Walking on Hot Ashes

Poetry

Sabat Beatto

Copyright

ISBN: 978-1-7337532-1-0
Walking on Hot Ashes - Poetry
Copyright © 2018 Sabat Beatto

TABLE OF CONTENTS

WALKING ON HOT ASHES

The stillness of night surrounds me.
I am being carried away, in a lucid dream.
Somehow, I lie in bed suspended,
in a state of in-between.
In a state of restless sleep as I ponder on my stark reality.
I know it's my mind's way of desperately hanging on to hope.
Its refusal to cope with my new sense of normalcy.
Consisting of unknown hotel rooms,
bed sheets, and foreign travel sized toiletries
that don't belong to me.

The aftermath of the fire still lives within me.
I still smell the stench of smoke.
Almost as if it's here - wafting the vents –
choking me.
It's burning my throat. Burning, burning,
burning...
I can hardly breathe.
Hardly breathe...

I want to cry out –
I deserve to vent too,
but all I see and feel is hot ashes and murky residue.
Suddenly, I know what I must do.
I must return to the home that I once knew.
This dream is telling me even if I don't believe,
I will confront what happened to me.
It can no longer have the power to haunt me.
When I finally accept it.
I'm slowly enveloped in a state of wakefulness and sleep.

Suddenly, I'm in front of the door, debating if I should go in.
But I don't know if I'll recover.

I'm sick to my stomach and truly shaken,
right down to my core.
I know what awaits me
beyond the threshold of the door.
But something stronger than myself demands that I must heal.
That I must dig down deep inside myself, be brave enough to feel.

I take a breath and prepare myself for what I'll find.
I'm brought back to a time
when this place looked and felt like mine.
Unlike the sight I see before me right now of shard fragments the fire
left behind.
I'm arrested when I feel my five senses come alive.

First, when I close my eyes,
visions of friends and family appears.

Next, I hear the echoes of laughter
and spontaneous glee reflecting a
perfect picture of a time when I was happy.

Then, I smell the aroma of my favorite meal.
The taste bursting upon my tongue,
causing me to sigh in anticipation because I know there's more to come.

Finally, I feel the warmth of home embracing me like a mother's touch.
I'm grateful that my senses were able to arouse me with those
unforgettable memories.
It means so much.
These are the heart shaped memories the fire dares not to steal.

Dream or not, or in-between, these moments feel so real.

This apartment held compartments of defining moments of my life.
Something goes off in me,
and I'm not willing to go down without a fight.
Even if I must walk through hot ashes and put it together brick by brick,
stone by stone,
I want to rest in the place that I used to call home.

Walking through hot ashes, unaware of the pain,
I'm not even conscious when my feet begin to ache.
Only the pursuit, and proving that this dream is a fallacy and untrue.
Where are you, God?
I really need you.

Walking on hot ashes, the intensity sears my soul.
If I let go, this dream becomes real and I have nowhere else to go.
God, can you hear me?
I feel like I lost everything.

My home was filled with treasures that grew to have meaning.
Mere possessions became objects of life lessons that formed tales so
bitter and sweet,
each day in this space of mine was well lived in.
Now those treasures dissolved into hot ashes at my feet.
But I don't want to admit defeat.
I'm not ready to surrender.
The soles of my feet
are blooded and blistered.

I reach down on my knees to gather scattered pieces.
As I feel myself shatter like broken glass.
I'm numb and don't have the answers,

so I look up toward heaven at last.
Don't tell me that it was all meant to be.
That I have no right to be upset and angry.
Or even a little guilty, though I have no idea why.

When the inner turmoil has settle down,
I know intuitively everything will be fine.
God tells me to let go now.
He will give me peace.
That I already salvaged from the wreckage what I truly need.
The thing that I was searching for lives inside of me.

I pick myself up from the floor,
clutching to this space no more.
Taking the key and locking the door.
I settle into sleep, finally succumbing to peace.
No longer am I lingering in a state of in-between.
For I know wherever I go, God is with me.
He has made me whole
and will guide me to my new home.

VEGAN CAGE

I want to take flight. I'm feeling caged in.
My mind, body and spirit are not in alignment.
My heart hasn't even processed what has happened.
I need nourishment that heals the soul and a change in scenery.
I can already feel the toll it's taken on my body.
I must break out this vegan cage.
Be liberated and free.
All the food in the room is stale or filled with burnt grease.

I'm inherently vegan and try to live my life green.
I recycle and I'm eco-friendly.
I believe in things being holistic and not being caught up in things.
That are ritualistic with lists and charts that flow.

Then everything shifted and then I realized,
that life had made plans of its own.
It's how I ended up here.
In this vacant hotel room all alone,
hungry and weak,
miles from my home.

I'm used to eating clean.
I eat food taken directly from the earth.
No living creature will I consume,
nor will I ever hurt.
If we are what we eat, then I know my worth.
The food we eat is supposed to
be restorative, not harmful in any way.
I will not compromise myself no matter
if things don't seem to be going my way.

When natural protein hits my palate by way of kale and dark leafy greens,
my appetite refuses be sedated by carnivorous red meat.
I stay away from dairy by making creamy cheese
out of cashews nuts and baking yeast.

I miss my tofu, soy milk and lentil beans.
I didn't assume this diet because of its popularity.
I am not vegan due to current trends in society.
I vowed to be healthy and now I'm filled with anxiety.
I have no kitchen to prepare my meals, and thus,
this is my reality.

I feel trapped – almost caged in.
I feel my body breaking down from within.
I know I'll soon need to go on a cleanse.
I feel like I need a detox. I'm suffering.
I must leave this suffocating box.
I need some reprieve.
Hopefully, I can find some peace and something good to eat.

When I venture out, on the street to enjoy the sweet night air,
I past small Bistros deli and food chains and think,
how decidedly unfair?
There's nowhere for me to eat
unless I want a hollow bun with no meat.

Just because "go vegan" is a hashtag or a tweet, doesn't make it cool.
I stop seeking acceptance way back in high school.
Most don't get it's a lifestyle.
It's not even about the food.
It's funny, how I'm suddenly in all this rage.
What am I to do?
My meal options are a few.

I feel constricted and I don't know what to do.

I want to take flight. I'm feeling caged in.
My mind, body and spirit are not in alignment.
My heart hasn't even processed what has happened.
I need nourishment that heals the soul and a change in scenery.
I can already feel the toll it's taken on my body.
I must break out this vegan cage.
Be liberated and free.
All the food in the room is stale
 or filled with burnt grease.

As I walk farther down the street,
I see a store that is familiar to me.
Right now, while I'm away from home,
 I just need a sense of community.
The menu has a section devoted to vegan dishes. At least for now,
I can grant one of my wishes.
And in a small way,
have become free.

A DAY

A day to forever remember,
yet, somewhat hard to forget.
The events are so vague in my mind.
For its the day I lost it all in a second.
I was never good with counting loses.
Not until the day I found I had uncountable loses.
I thank the Lord for sparing us.
But that's not enough to heal the pain

MY LESSONS

I've learned a lot since my youth.
Like how to count and how to muse.
But the lessons I got never included.
How do I deal with so much pain and so much grief?
How do I deal with the loss of all my favorite things?
My favorite shirt, my baseball cap,
my scented perfumes.
They are all just ashes remain in the deadly,
unforgivable fumes.
I learnt about friends and how a smile can change a mood.
I learnt to be thankful for what I have and to be good.

THE PAIN

After the fire, I learned to love the silence.
I can't wear headphones anymore,
because I want to listen for the fire sirens.
I can no longer wear heavy perfume,
in case I smell smoke.
My luggage is half empty,
so I don't have to keep anything I can't carry.
I sleep with one eye closed and one eye open,
just to be ready anytime.
I am usually paranoid –
where are my keys,
my old sweater,
where is it?
Where is my baseball cards collection,
the Yankee cup?
The papers of my car, my passport,
where is my TV,
my laptop, the usb, my favorite books?
The bird can't sing no more,
where is the mic?

COMING TO TERMS

Now that I know I lost almost everything in the fire,
I have my most prized possessions,
my family right here.
But what of the childhood photos of my son?
What of the couch I worked so hard to pay off?
I can't begin to count the losses I see.
I feel hurt,
like a part of me died in the fire.
They may just be material things,
but to me, it was more.
It was the significance of something that felt like a dream.

THE CHANGES

With everything but our lives gone,
I turned to charity to help me through the dawn.
Once upon a time,
I slept in a bed so warm.
Now, I must squeeze tight just to feel the warmth.
Things will be back to normal for us eventually.
But nothing will ever feel the same actually.
For I wanted so much from the little I had gathered.
I wanted to make memories.
Live.
Grow old in that place.
But I now know how it feels to lose it all.
I used to be someone with a good and loving home.
Now it's all gone.

LOOKING IN FROM THE OUTSIDE

People try to tell me how lucky I am.
I know for sure,
I am a blessed man indeed.
I have no permanent physical scar to remind me of that time.
I have no bruise or loss to cry over all the time.
But how can I go on building if it can all turn to ashes within the next minute?
I know nothing will ever be like it once was, that's a given fact.
But looking in from the outside, I can't help but ask what if.
I am not complaining,
I am grateful in fact.
I just know things will never be as it were.

THANK YOU, GOD

Where do I even begin dear Lord?
If it weren't for you,
I wouldn't have been up.
If it weren't for your care,
my son would have remained asleep.
I would have watched my family die,
being scared and helpless.
Thank you, a million times over,
for everything dear lord.
Thank you for my life and for the loss I have incurred.
Thank you for your mercy and sparing our lives.
Thank you so much, God, I owe you a lot!

GOODBYE TO THE OLD

I will miss the old house and all the memories in it;
where I put my favorite chair and watched every show;
where my son took his first steps.
I will miss the curtains and my favorite picture on the wall.
I will miss the smell of coming home to a freshly cooked meal.
I will miss the laughter we shared there and the friends we hosted.
I will miss my collections and all the secrets they held.
I will miss the old apartment as I move on to the new and bare one.

HELLO NEW, GOODBYE OLD.

I never thought I'd be starting over like this.
I can never fully let go,
but I can try for my kid.
There are a lot of things that I will miss.
There are a lot of things that I will always remember.
I just pray that this new journey will be worthwhile.
That each moment I live will be better than the last.
That the new hello will bring about many blessings,
and the goodbye I say to the old will help me forget.
I will forever remain grateful through the good and the bad.

BURNED BY FIRE

Burned by fire, flooded with regret .
Blown away by the magnitude of the events,
I won't ever forget.
Grounded by my family,
they're all I have left.
As much as I will miss my things,
they're all I really need.

DANCING

One step forward and one step back is a dance I always do.
Scared to leave it all behind.
Scared to move toward something new.

THE MEMORY

My lungs fill with smoke
and my breathing becomes labored.
The memory takes me back to when my sense of security wavered.
Cheeks burning red, eyes filled with tears
Scared to inhale as I try to swallow the fear of losing everything
I've built for years.

US

I reached for your picture and realized I didn't have it.
I didn't have anything.
All that remained of a life well lived was us.

EVERYTHING IS GONE

I can see the flames imprinted in my brain,
dancing and taunting me as they take with glee,
almost everything that meant anything to me.

NEVER TAKE MY MEMORIES

I could grieve for an hour or for a day, but in the end,
it's gone.
It'll never be the same again.
Replacements may come,
but they can never replace the memories.
Yet, neither can they burn them away.

LIVE AGAIN

Is this a lesson?
What must I learn?
Perhaps just to live again
after watching my whole life burn?

MATERIALISTIC

I wish I could say that I am not materialistic.

That stuff is all it is,

but I cannot.

I feel emotionally connected to what is and what was mine.

Don't you dare try to belittle those feelings.

KEEP MOVING

I know that I must keep moving forward and
I am so grateful that I am able to do so.

SOMETHINGS CAN'T BE LOST

I lost my hope, I lost my mind,
I lost my place to live.
What I didn't lose was my heart, my soul,
or all the love I have to give

NIGHTMARES

What is this horrible nightmare I have woken up to?
I blink and wipe my eyes in total disbelief.
I can't seem to wake up because
I see now that I am already awake.
This is not a dream.
This is my new reality.

NEVER AGAIN

I cannot explain the emotions that came over me,
a heartbreak like no other.
I will never again get to cut that grass.
I will never again get to sit on that porch.
I will never again see my collections or my favorite clothes.
I will never see those childhood photos.
The simple things I've done so many times before,
I will never again get to do.
Never again. Never again...

EXCUSE ME

Excuse me while I move past this.

Let me pack up my troubles and slide on by.

I wouldn't want to make you uncomfortable by having to witness my pain.

Allow me to get over this quickly,

because there is no use in crying over spilled milk, right?

So excuse me while I put away my vulnerability so you can feel better about your insensitivity.

NAKED

I feel stripped and naked even though I'm not.
"It's all just stuff."
That stuff has covered me and made me feel safe.
Stuff that I used to put my son to bed with.
Stuff that comforted me when no one could Stuff that held my secrets and my memories.
Stuff that nursed my family to health when we were sick.
Stuff that I got used to and that got used to me.
Stuff that was a part of the person I am.
Stuff that my tears fell for.
That stuff will never be "just stuff".

WHO AM I?

Who am I?

Or better yet, who was I?

With all the reminders of who I was buried under ash and soot,

how am I supposed to know who I am meant to be?

Who am I without my favorite chair?

The one that made me forget about my problems every time I sat down.

Or my favorite hat that made me feel so confident,

I thought I could be a movie double.

Do I continue to be who I always was

or do I use this as an opportunity to become someone new?

Maybe I'm the guy with the new golf clubs that's off every Sunday

without my old things surrounding me,

telling me who I am.

Maybe, I can finally become who I've always wanted to be.

DEAR FIRE

Dear Fire,

I see you for what you really are.
A challenge and a lesson.
Sweeping through my life,
leaving behind destruction in your wake.
A challenge to keep moving forward.
Teaching me that life is a fragile thing and nothing lasts forever.

Thank you... for nothing..

HOME

Home is a feeling
and stuff reminds us of that feeling.
Home is also where the heart is and mine is with my family.
So, although I may have lost my house,
I will never lose my true home.

SEIZE THE DAY

We should always strive to have our living spaces reflect who we are, not who we were in the past.
I shall seize this opportunity.

WHAT IT TOOK

The fire didn't just take away my things,
it also took with it my sense of security; my stability;
my safety nets; my landing zone.
No matter how many times I close my eyes,
I see my stuff is gone.
How do I begin to repair the emotional damage that is left to take its place?
How will I look at tomorrow and the uncertainties I will face?

ALLOWING

I allowed myself to feel bad
and to release the emotions inside.
I allowed myself to get up and fall again.
I accepted the tears I cried.
I allowed myself to feel in control and out of control.
I allowed myself to hide.
I accepted my life was a roller coaster I allowed myself to ride.

BRAVE FACE

When everything first happened,
I wanted to be alone to dwell in the sorrow and pity that comes with losing my home.
But I knew I couldn't do that.
I could never be so selfish.
I had my family to look after and my community outreach.
So many people were there for me and I had to be there too.
I wanted to step up and show a brave face for everyone we knew.

NO WORDS

At first, it was hard to talk about,
I could barely find the words.
It would get caught in my throat
and became afraid to make their way out.
So many thoughts overwhelmed my mind.
I couldn't keep them straight.
Feelings consumed me,
and they were different all the time.
Things are a bit easier now.
The words come and go,
but I am still waiting for the day when again,
they start to flow.

PERSON ON TV

It could never happen to me,
it only happens to people on tv.
The ones that weren't careful, the ones that least expected it.
They always say it tearfully.
And yet, it did happen to me.
I was just as unprepared,
not wanting to admit such things were more common than I'd feared.

CRAZY LIKE A FOX

They say this experience can be life changing.
And they are right about that.
Not in the way they think though.
It's akin to being crazy like a fox,
in that I have changed.
But I haven't changed,
the things around me has changed the most.

TETHERED

For moment in time I felt a thought.
I were no longer tethered to the earth.
I felt weightless.
It felt good and weird,
almost like a relief.
How could I feel so good about something so terrible though?
So, I come crashing back down and allow the pain back inside.
This is how it's supposed to be.

BRICK BY BRICK

We will have to rebuild our lives from the ground up,
brick by brick,
with a strong foundation like an Egyptian pyramid.
This time around we can make it better,
brick by brick.
Then fill it with more new memories.
The best parts of our lives aren't over.
They have yet to come.
This time we will keep our memories safe inside our pyramid,
brick by brick.

CLOUDED

Dark clouds of smoke hang heavy
as though a thunderstorm is about to begin.
Only this time, they do not surround my house.
They surround my head instead,
with a clouded mind and a heavy heart.
I don't know what next to do.
I look towards my family,
They are like a ray of sun poking through.

NO ROUND TWO

Feeling defeated and emotionally depleted.
Never wanting to fight fire with fire,
side fire fought, and it won.
Even after its victory,
it continued to rage on until there wasn't anything left.
Reigning undefeated.
Praying there would not be a rematch.
I don't want my loss repeated.

VALUE

When thinking about your possessions,
try not to put too much value in material things.
No matter how much you may like them,
or the comfort they may bring.
We might think we love them and that's not a love we choose,
but it'll be much harder when everything you love,
becomes everything you lose.

ACT NOW

When the only thing you can do is cry and beg
and plead and wonder why,
it is then that you must do something.

ANYTHING

You must not dwell in sorrow.
The lowest points make the best times to build a
better tomorrow.

LET IT GO

Think of all you had
and what you did to get it.
Be grateful for its time and let it go.
There is something better waiting for your attention.

REPLACEMENT

I had taken many things for granted and probably still would.
It's funny how we don't realize we'll
miss something until we no longer have it.
This time around,
I will own things with intention.
I'm sure I don't remember half the things that were taken away from me.
But the things I do remember had a special place with me.
Those are the only things I will need replace.

FAMILY

Sleeping on a park bench or bathing in the ocean,
as long as I have my family,
I am still more blessed than I could be.

I'D RATHER

I'd rather lose my stuff than lose myself.

HOME

Son,

I thought the four walls to be home.

But walls fall and leave only hope.

I hope you are much wiser than I so you can see what I couldn't;

that home is in the people you love.

PHOENIX

The fire that was once our warmth,
a spark that illuminated the dark,
became the tongues that licked away at my pride.
Charring the sweat of my brow to vapor and ash.
Yet here we sit by it,
as our memories are reborn in the flames,
dancing before our eyes.
Melting our love together,
stronger than ever now.
Glowing even brighter,
like a phoenix.

TRUST

Never trust in the world a trust that stands proud.
The walls of our house
became the ground for fate's thrusts.
Surely like human nature changes,
tearing down our securities,
and burning down the walls of our achievements.
Trust most in yourself.

MOMENTS

Every day life is changing.
But moments are life's defining.
Never leaving you the same,
broken or stronger.
Always testing or questioning your mettle as a man.
All you need to be, is human.
For lessons will present themselves in the thick of the experience.
Live in your moments.

ALIVE

The flames were bright
and had never looked so alive.
Dancing to the song only they knew, and I heard them say
"burn, baby burn".
I knew I'd live,
but wondered if I'll ever feel alive.
How I hated the flames,
hurt by their joy at my loss.
Jealous of their freedom in that moment,
I learned the only valuable I have left.
We are free, we are most alive.

FAMILY

It was my very own judgement day and the flames were my hell.

But the life of family was my saving grace.

Their love was my salvation.

Their presence is my hope.

Now I can face tomorrow,

because I have faith in my family.

We all need family.

POSSESSIONS

The fire took away everything;
my favorites; the valuables; and even the chores.
It swept away my world, it didn't withhold.
I wept, I could no longer hold.
Standing there with ash in my mouth,
and the heat of destruction all around,
I swear I never felt so cold.
My possessions were gone,
both the prized and obsolete.
What I couldn't see was that all I owned remained untouched.
My memories, love, and family.
Know the difference,
and which is more valuable.
It took loss for me to remember.

THE DARKNESS

It was so bright all around me.
For once I wished I wasn't standing in the light.
It was hot and blinding,
making merry and away with all that was mine.
It danced in delight,
blazing, but not illuminating.
I could see no path,
only destruction.
In the blaze of fire,
I found a darkness and a truth.
True light comes from within.

SCARRED

As the fire took its last breath,
clinging desperately to its short existence,
I realized I'd never be the same again.
I was cut, hurt,
and bleeding.
A piece of me was the debris and ash that filled the night sky and my lungs.
I was breathing my last,
and it was torture to think I had something kindred with the fire.
Nature's killer-for-hire,
fate's very own squire.
I felt like coal for karma's fire.
This was not a dream,
but still it was a nightmare,
a reality that will leave me marred.
Scarred.

MUSINGS

Some days it feels like a noose,
round my neck never lose.
This loss, the hurt, the pain,
life didn't let me choose.
Everybody looks from the outside: seeing, thinking, feeling,
but not understanding.
I wonder if I know who I am.
If this was destiny or just a tragedy.
Was this meant to be?
Or is it just a flaw in the system?
Heaven give me an answer, nature reward me,
I demand my karma.
My thoughts and feelings brew in a toxic mix.
Then I remember family
and my anger melts in their love.
Only to harden like wax in my lonely hours.
But my strength still stands,
drawing from my faith, supported by hope.
And I pray,
grateful for life and the chance it offers to be better.